This library edition published in 2012 by Walter Foster Publishing, Inc.
Distributed by Black Rabbit Books.
P.O. Box 3263 Mankato, Minnesota 56002

Designed and published by Walter Foster Publishing, Inc.
Walter Foster is a registered trademark.

Printed in Mankato, Minnesota, USA by CG Book Printers, a division of Corporate Graphics.

First Library Edition

Library of Congress Cataloging-in-Publication Data

Watch me draw Disney's Mickey Mouse clubhouse / illustrated by the Disney
Storybook Artists ; step-by-step drawing illustrations by Elizabeth
Runyen. -- 1st Library Edition.
     pages cm
  ISBN 978-1-936309-74-0
  1. Cartoon characters--Juvenile literature. 2. Mickey Mouse
(Fictitious character)--Juvenile literature. 3.
Drawing--Technique--Juvenile literature. I. Runyen, Elizabeth,
illustrator. II. Disney Storybook Artists, illustrator.
  NC1764.W376 2012
  741.5'1--dc23
                              2012004273

052012
17679

9 8 7 6 5 4 3 2 1

DISNEY
MICKEY MOUSE
CLUBHOUSE

Illustrated by the Disney Storybook Artists

Step-by-Step Drawing Illustrations by Elizabeth Runyen

Hello everybody, I'm Mickey Mouse! And I have a whole list of items I'd like to learn to draw. Can you help me? Together is better! But what should we start with? Look up, look down, look all around—what do you see? I know, flowers!

the Flower Spot

Flowers
Kite
Fish
Pizza Slice
Crab
Toucan
Sandcastle
Alarm Clock
Penguin
Crown
Lizard

Come on, let's draw the flowers!

When the grass is green and the sky is blue, it's great to be outdoors, hanging with your pals! I like to mow the lawn and Minnie likes to plant flowers. What's Goofy doing? Raise your hand if you know the answer. Yep, that's right—flying a kite!

Come on, let's draw the kite!

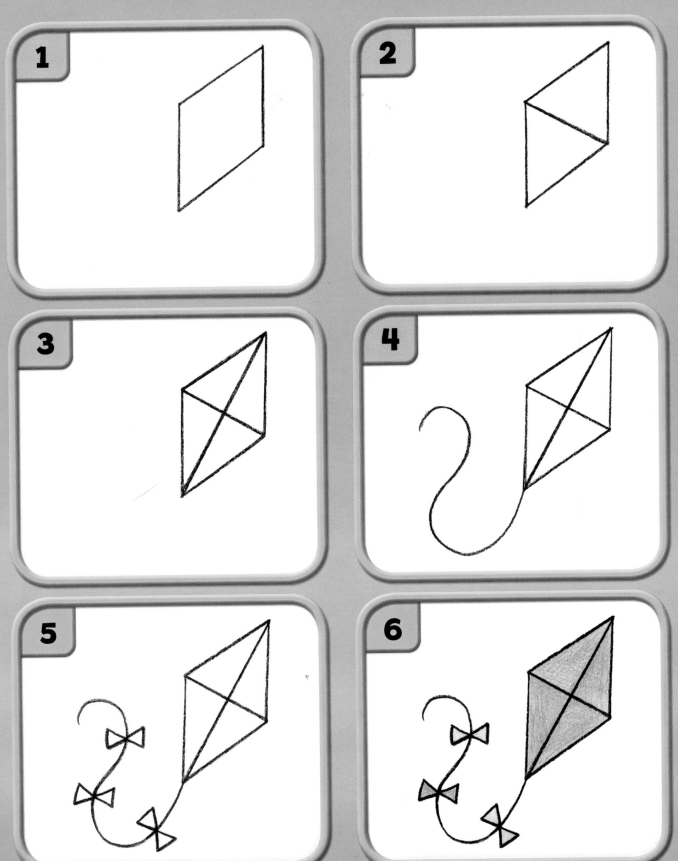

What should we draw? I can see the wheels turning! What do you see? I see a lot of things: Lightning bugs, turtles, pussy willows, and even fish. Do you think you can draw a fish? Oh, boy—let's try!

Come on, let's draw the fish!

Come on inside! It's time to eat. Oh, boy, look at all the food—
sandwiches, spaghetti with meatballs, pie, cherries, and
pepperoni pizza! Pizza is one of my favorite foods.
What's your favorite food?

Come on, let's draw the pizza slice!

Together is better, which is why I love to travel with friends.
The beach is the perfect place to play and meet new pals.
Want to come along? Let's go! You might meet a dolphin,
a seagull, a sea star, or a family of crabs!

Come on, let's draw the crab!

1

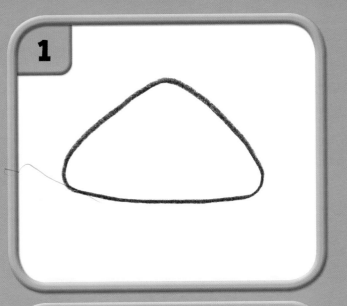

2

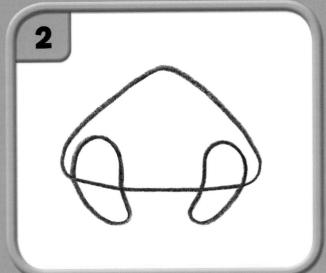

3

4

5

6

In the rainforest, there are a lot of green plants and trees!
The snakes are also green, but the birds are bright and colorful!
Do you see four parrots and one toucan? Good job! I love it when
birds sing a happy song with a sweet tweet, tweet.

Come on, let's draw the toucan!

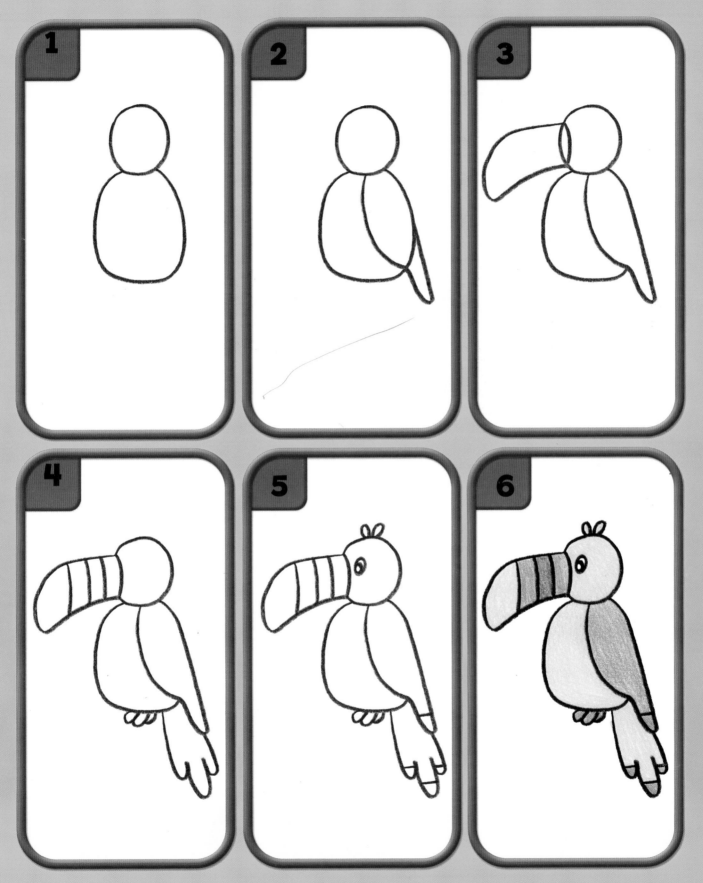

Hot dog! It's always fun to spend time at the beach! Would you rather splash around in the water or build a sandcastle? Hey, I bet that you can do better than build a sandcastle— you can draw one.

Come on, let's draw the sandcastle!

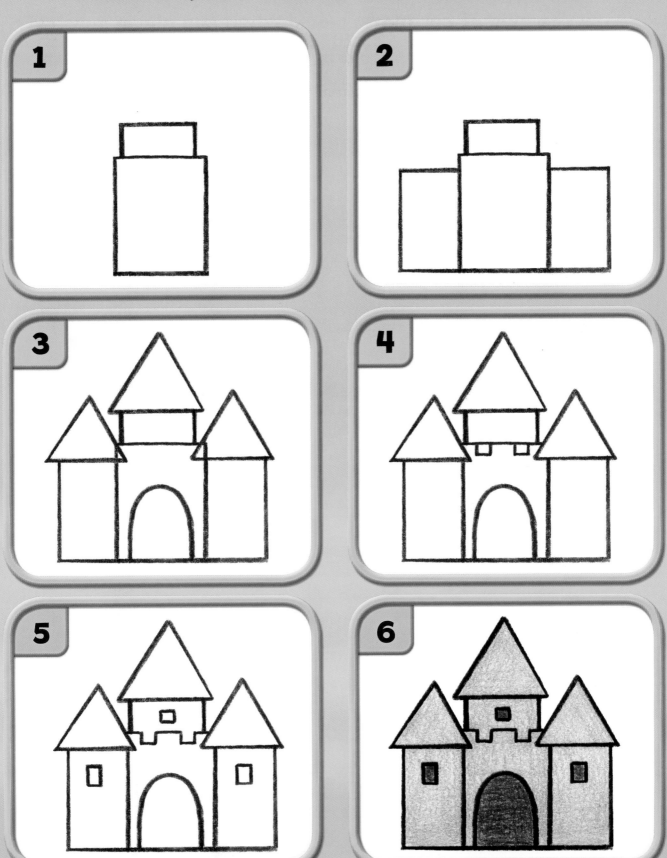

Rise and shine! Minnie loves waking up early in the morning with the help of her alarm clock! When the alarm goes off, she greets the day with a big smile. Now it's your turn! Draw an alarm clock just like Minnie's.

Come on, let's draw the alarm clock!

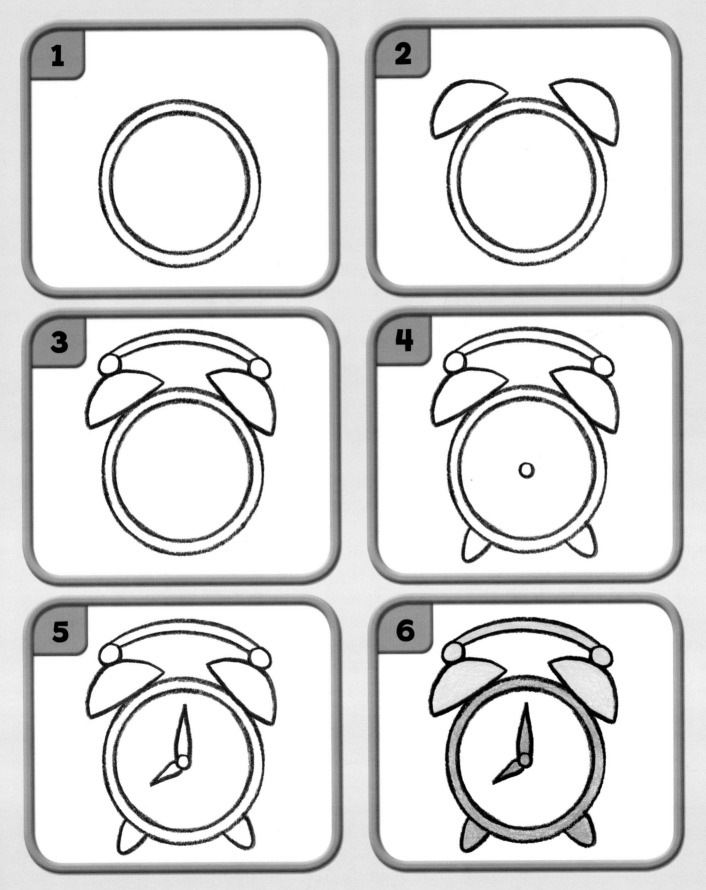

Here comes Pluto, looking for fun—along with a few new friends! Meeska, Mooska, Mickey Mouse—Pluto is surrounded by penguins! What do you think? Good idea! Let's draw one of Pluto's new friends.

Come on, let's draw the penguin!

Are you ready to play? Let's play dress-up in the hat shop! I'm looking for a hat made for a king. Do you see a crown? There it is! It's gold and it has four points. Help me draw it.

Come on, let's draw the crown!

1
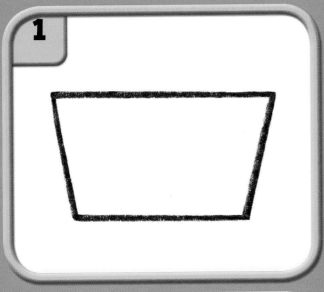

2

3

4

5

6

It looks like Minnie has found some new friends out in the desert: two cute little lizards! They have polka dots on their skin that are like the dots on Minnie's bow. Do you think you can draw a lizard? Go ahead, jump in!

Come on, let's draw the lizard!

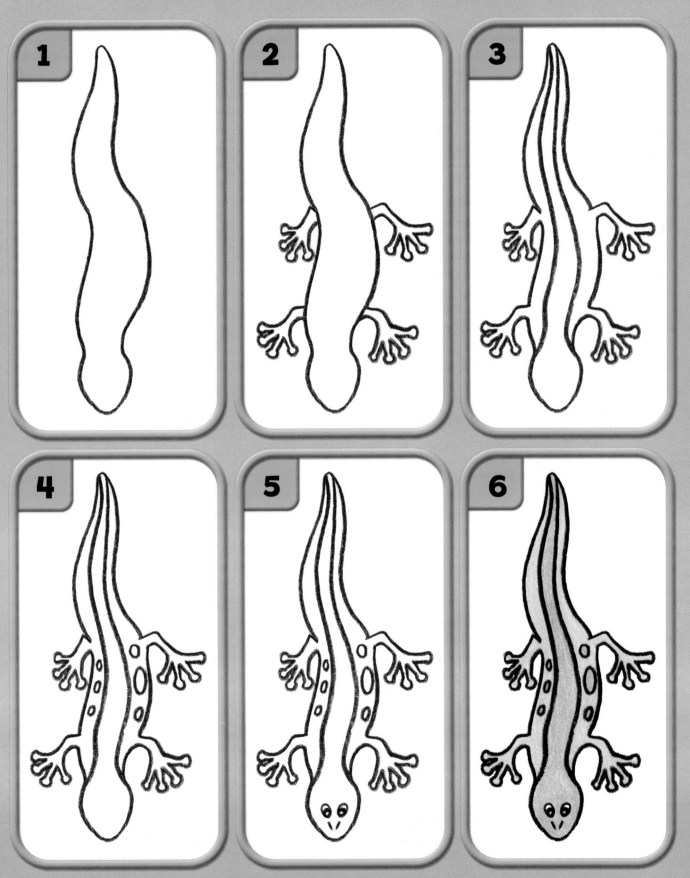

Super cheers! You've learned to draw so many things!
But the fun doesn't have to end. Look around for
new things to draw and keep drawing!